YOU CAN DO IT !

·Things You Can Do To
READ
THE BIBLE
PRAYERFULLY

MARK W. LOVE

CONCORDIA PUBLISHING HOUSE · SAINT LOUIS

Copyright © 2013 Concordia Publishing House
3558 S. Jefferson Ave., St. Louis, MO 63118-3968
1-800-325-3040 · www.cph.org

Quotations marked *TLSB* are taken from the original articles or notes of *The Lutheran Study Bible*, copyright © 2009 by Concordia Publishing House. All rights reserved.

Scripture quotations are from The Holy Bible, English Standard Version, copyright © 2001 by Crossway Bibles, a division of Good News Publishers. Used by permission. All rights reserved.

Catechism quotations are taken from *Luther's Small Catechism with Explanation*, copyright © 1986, 1991 Concordia Publishing House. All rights reserved.

Quote from *A Simple Way to Pray* is from Martin Luther, *A Simple Way to Pray*. Translated by Matthew C. Harrison, copyright © 2012 Concordia publishing House. All rights reserved.

Manufactured in the United States of America

1 2 3 4 5 6 7 8 9 10   22 21 20 19 18 17 16 15 14 13

TABLE OF CONTENTS

Have you ever wanted something badly only to realize you weren't willing to do what it took to get it? We want to lose weight, but we don't want to exercise or change our eating habits. We want the current government services and maybe more, but we don't want to pay higher taxes to get them. In all aspects of life in this fallen world, we struggle to attain desired outcomes while avoiding the very means of achieving them. Even our spiritual life of faith in Christ is not exempt. We want to be closer to the Lord and more faithful in our walk of life, but often we'd rather bypass the paths to Him found in His Word and Sacraments.

We want to be close to God. We want to be faithful. Still, we search for the minimum we have to do. How much do I need to read the Bible? How often do I need to worship? How long do my prayers need to be? These questions resonate with the same tone as Peter's, "How often will my brother sin against me, and I forgive him?" (Matthew 18:21). When our life in Jesus Christ becomes a checklist to be okay or right with the Lord, we are no longer living by faith in Christ. If you're focused on having to read the Bible so much, pray so much, and worship so much to be right with the Lord, you're not seeking the Lord for what He has done to save you. You're seeking what you believe He would have you do to be acceptable to Him. All your spiritual and religious activities become nothing but a chasing after, with the hopes of doing just enough of the right things to make yourself good enough to receive God's blessings. The Bible becomes a spiritual checklist of all the things you must be and do to maintain your rightness with God. This makes reading the Bible, prayer, and worship purely matters of the Law: if you do *x*, then God does *y*.

As blessed as the Law of God is, we have been given a better word in the Gospel of Jesus Christ. "For the law was given through Moses; grace and truth came through Jesus Christ" (John 1:17). Jesus brings, gives, and works the grace of God that always does for us what we cannot do to be right with God. From the moment of His conception to His rest in the tomb, Jesus did and suffered all for us to take away our sins and justify us before God. This is His grace, as explained in Ephesians 2:1–10:

> And you were dead in the trespasses and sins in which you once walked, following the course of this world, following the prince of the power of the air, the spirit that is now at work in the sons of disobedience— among whom we all once lived in the passions of our flesh, carrying out the desires of the body and the mind, and were by nature children of wrath, like the rest of mankind. But God, being rich in mercy, because of the great love with which He loved us, even when we were dead in our trespasses, made us alive together with Christ—by grace you have been saved—and raised us up with Him and seated us with Him in the

heavenly places in Christ Jesus, so that in the coming ages He might show the immeasurable riches of His grace in kindness toward us in Christ Jesus. For by grace you have been saved through faith. And this is not your own doing; it is the gift of God, not a result of works, so that no one may boast. For we are His workmanship, created in Christ Jesus for good works, which God prepared beforehand, that we should walk in them.

Having been saved and changed by His grace alone, we read the Bible differently. No longer do we read merely for a checklist of what we ought to do. Now we read the Bible for the saving list of what the Lord has done and what He continues to do, what He gives and what He works now to bring us under His Gospel.

The words of James 4:8 don't mean we have to act first to earn God's attention. It simply tells us where to receive the gifts God has for us: near to Him. This is the joy of the incarnation— of Christ becoming flesh and being born a helpless child—God came near to us so we can be near to Him and His heavenly Father.

The Lord tells the baptized in James 4:8, "Draw near to God, and He will draw near to you." Moreover, if anyone, believer or unbeliever, wishes to draw near to God, there is one sure place to find Him: "the Word became flesh and dwelt among us, and we have seen His glory, glory as of the only Son from the Father, full of grace and truth" (John 1:14). The Word of God is Jesus Christ. Jesus Christ is the Word of God. If you would draw near to God, then you must draw near to the Word of God, Jesus Christ. To draw near to the Lord is to seek Him who has sought, found, and saved you. Through Scripture, Baptism, and the Lord's Supper, the Word—the Lord—seeks to strengthen and enlighten your faith. Reading the Bible is one way to seek the Lord, to receive Him in His word of Law and His saving word of Gospel.

While this sounds simple, it is often not. If you're like the rest of us, you likely make it difficult for yourself to draw near and hear the Lord. How so?

First, even though you have been born again with a deep desire to draw near and listen to God, this new life must compete with your sinful nature. Praying and reading the Bible are contrary to the desires of your old sinful nature, which is hostile to all things of God (Romans 8:7). When you take time to listen to God and more time to pray, you have to bring your sinful nature kicking and screaming because it refuses to submit to God or His Word. It's like the annoying passenger in the back of the car asking every few minutes, "Are we there yet?" However, only through the Word of God is the sinful nature suppressed and silenced. So read on!

Second, listening and responding according to what you have heard from God takes time and effort. In a world that runs by the clock, any beneficial, prayerful reading of the Bible takes time. Reading the Bible isn't like social media where God posts something and you post something back. The people of Isaiah's day actually thought that such a shallow

7

relationship with God was okay. "This people draw near with their mouth and honor Me with their lips, while their hearts are far from Me" (Isaiah 29:13). The Lord knew this temptation in the hearts of His people then and today, which is why He goes on to promise, "I will again do wonderful things with this people, with wonder upon wonder" (v. 14).

All the wonderful things the Lord did with His people then and the wonderful things He does today are always done through His Word. May the Holy Spirit draw near to you as you draw near to God in His Word and prayer.

What follows are five different things you can do to better read God's Word and understand His work taking place in what you read. Each will offer ways for you to respond to the Lord according to what He has said. In this way, you can continue the conversation the Lord began as you read His Word.

Have you ever spoken with someone you considered important? Did thoughts race through your mind of what to say and how to say it? I have been there and done that more times than I care to count. Most people who know ahead of time that they will be speaking with someone they believe to be important prepare what they are going to say or ask. How many of us, though, spend time preparing ourselves to listen?

We read the Bible to learn what the Lord has to say, yet we struggle to really *listen*. How many times have you concluded your reading of the Bible without having heard anything that sticks with you or enlightened you? This experience isn't so different from our daily lives. How often has your spouse or child heard your words without really listening to what you said? How often have you listened poorly? So, what most interferes with being listened to in these situations? I have learned that my family listens and understands best when the television, the computer, the game, and the like are off. With any of these distractions, my words risk becoming lost among the many words they are taking in at that same moment.

Adults do this as well. Our workdays are filled with the noise of e-mail, colleagues, schedules, and deadlines. In order to focus on one thing, we need to remove ourselves from the noise. You can do this by literally turning things off or, better yet, getting away from everything to a quiet place.

While we may be able to lessen the external noise, we cannot get away from ourselves. None of us can escape the mental, emotional, and physical noise that fills our hearts and minds. Although we have been eternally redeemed and born again in Christ through Baptism, we still have our sinful nature, which is hostile to God. It does not, will not, and cannot submit to the Word of God (Romans 8:7). While the Holy Spirit leads and moves you to read the Bible, your sinful nature is totally against this desire (see Galatians 5:17). It will crank up the volume of any mental, emotional, and physical noises to interfere with listening to God. The question then becomes how to turn down the noise from within.

We cannot ever deal with sin in any of its forms. The apostle Paul confesses this reality:

> I have the desire to do what is right, but not the ability to carry it out. For I do not do the good I want, but the evil I do not want is what I keep on doing. Now if I do what I do not want, it is no longer I who do it, but sin that dwells within me. So I find it to be a law that when I want to do right, evil lies close at hand. . . . Wretched man that I am! Who will deliver me from this body of death? Thanks be to God through Jesus Christ our Lord! (Romans 7:18–21, 24–25)

The way you can turn down the sinful noise so that you might hear and listen to what the Lord would say is by calling on the name of the Lord (Psalm 50:15).

To pray in faith is to bow and bend your heart to God. In this you acknowledge your need for His mercy and grace to do for you what you cannot do and His gracious supply to meet your needs. Whenever you exercise yourself in faith, doing that which the Lord has set you free to do, your sinful nature is suppressed and subjugated to the work of the Holy Spirit. To exercise yourself in privilege of prayer doesn't save you from your sinful nature, but the Holy Spirit does turn down the volume of the sinful nature's noise for you. What could you pray to suppress the sinful noises within yourself and prepare to listen?

Luther's Small Catechism with Explanation says, "Prayer is speaking to God in words and thoughts" (p. 174). This leads many to think that prayer is one of the easiest and most natural things the believer can do. While prayer is to be simple and straightforward, that does not make it easy or natural. This is illustrated by a request the disciples made to Jesus: "Lord, teach us to pray" (Luke 11:1). Of all the things the disciples asked of Jesus, prayer is the only thing they asked Him to teach them. Jesus then gave them the blessed prayer we refer to as the Lord's Prayer (see Luke 11:2–4). What is striking in the prayer Jesus gives is that He teaches the disciples and us more than simply what to pray. Jesus teaches the perspective from which each of us is to approach God in prayer, as a child to his or her Father, as one under He who is over all. Each petition or request that follows is also an implied confession of our need and of what only He can supply to us. This prayer from Jesus remains the best for the whole of our life in Christ, spiritual and physical.

Long before the Lord taught the Lord's Prayer, He taught the people of Israel, His disciples, and us how to pray about the Word of God in the words of Psalm 119. The divine arrangement of its 22 stanzas follows each letter of the Hebrew alphabet. Each stanza is composed of eight verses, which points the prayer to the new creation. The number 8 is used in both the Old and New Testaments. In His covenant with the people of Israel, the Lord commanded that all males be circumcised on the eighth day (Leviticus 12:3). Circumcision designated the child as one who belonged to God and to whom belonged all of God's promises (Word) about the coming Messiah. Christ speaks of the eight Beatitudes (Matthew 5), which all speak of our life in Him now, while pointing to our life in the new creation. Perhaps the main thing that ties the number 8 to the new creation is the fact that our Lord rose on the eighth day. The resurrection of Christ took place on Sunday, which was the eighth day, or the beginning of the new cre-

This isn't, of course, the only place Jesus speaks about prayer. Matthew 7:7 also confesses both our need and that God is the only one who can and will supply it. "Ask, and it will be given to you; seek, and you will find; knock, and it will be opened to you."

ation. Everyone who is born again is born through the Word of God. This makes the Word of God the source of our life in Christ. Therefore, Psalm 119, which is about the Word of God, is the prayer of every believer as we read the Bible.

When praying the stanzas of Psalm 119, you will find that it uses different words to refer to God's Word. Each of these supports and serves the understanding of the psalm. (Note: Italics are added to the following passages from Psalm 119 to highlight these key words.)

"Blessed are those whose way is blameless, who walk in the *law* of the Lᴏʀᴅ!" (Psalm 119:1)

law "Instruction" or "direction," including God's Commandments as well as His proclamation of love and mercy in the Messiah, Jesus. . . . The [Law] provides God's instruction and truth, which guide our steps in all situations. (*TLSB*, p. 971)

In the first verse, we acknowledge that one is blessed who walks in the *law* (the instruction or direction) of the Lord. So when praying this verse before reading the Bible, you are acknowledging your need to walk in the *law*, the instruction, the direction of God's words.

"Blessed are those who keep His *testimonies*, who seek Him with their whole heart." (Psalm 119:2)

testimonies The "witnesses" of the covenant. The ten "words" written on the tablets of the Law (Exodus 20:2–17), which Moses stored in the ark of the covenant. [These 10 "words" are the Ten Commandments.] (*TLSB*, p. 971)

Here you acknowledge that one is blessed who seeks the Lord in His *testimonies* (the Ten Commandments/the will of God) with all his or her heart. So when praying this verse before reading the Bible, you acknowledge your need to seek the Lord with all your heart in His *testimonies* as are found in the Bible, the Word of God.

"You have commanded Your *precepts* to be kept diligently." (Psalm 119:4)

precepts Things "deserving attention," "appointed for observation" (the verb means "to visit" or "attend to"). Each teaching of God's precious Word deserves the attention of His people. (*TLSB*, p. 971)

In this verse you acknowledge that the Lord has commanded that His *precepts* (things deserving attention because He spoke or did them) must be kept diligently. So when praying this verse before reading the Bible, you acknowledge the need to diligently keep His *precepts* as may be found in His Word.

"Oh that my ways may be steadfast in keeping Your *statutes*!" (Psalm 119:5)

statutes Thing[s] "prescribed" or "due." . . . Things written as decrees [as something ordered]. (*TLSB*, p. 971)

Here you acknowledge that you need to be steadfast in keeping the Lord's *statutes* (things prescribed or ordered for you to do). Because this is a statement declaring what you need, it is also a confession of what you lack and a confession of faith in the Lord to provide what you lack. So when praying this verse before reading the Bible, you are acknowledging three things: (1) the need for your ways to be steadfast in keeping the Lord's *statutes*; (2) your inability to do this rightly; and (3) your faith in the Lord to save you through His Word.

> **"Then I shall not be put to shame, having my eyes fixed on all Your *commandments*." (Psalm 119:6)**

commandments Things "charged," "commanded," or "commissioned" by the Lord. (*TLSB*, p. 971)

Here you acknowledge that if you have your eyes fixed on all God's *commandments* (things you have been charged or commanded to do by Him), you will not be put to shame. So when praying this verse before reading the Bible, you are acknowledging your need to diligently keep His *commandments* as may be found in what you are about to read.

> **"I will praise You with an upright heart, when I learn Your righteous *rules*." (Psalm 119:7)**

rules "Judgments." A legal term for the decisions of a judge. This can include rules to be followed as well as declarations of freedom and innocence. Therefore, the term frequently describes justification and God's mercy. (*TLSB*, p. 971)

Here you acknowledge that only when you learn the Lord's righteous *rules* (His decisions of judgment and mercy) will you be able to praise Him with an upright heart. So when praying this verse before reading the Bible, you are acknowledging your need to learn the Lord's righteous *rules* as may be found in what you are about to read.

"How can a young man keep his way pure? By guarding it according to Your *word*." (Psalm 119:9)

word Something "spoken." Used for all manner of messages (edicts, reports, commands, promises) or a "matter" about which one speaks. (*TLSB*, p. 971)

Here you acknowledge that the only way for anyone to keep his or her way pure is by guarding or attending to their living according to God's Word. (Word is understood as what the Lord has literally spoken through prophets, Christ, or apostles and what He has further inspired the holy writers to write concerning history, wisdom, and other accounts.) So when praying this verse, you are acknowledging your need to guard and attend to the living of your life according to the Word of God you are about to read.

"Plead my cause and redeem me; give me life according to Your *promise*." (Psalm 119:154)

promises "Utterances" or "sayings," especially those of command or promise. When the saying involves fulfillment, "promise" is the preferred translation. *TLSB*, p. 971)

Here you acknowledge that you are unable to redeem yourself or even to speak your own case. God's Word, in the person of His Son, speaks for us. His blood pleads to God on our behalf (Hebrews 12:24). Apart from God's Word, we have no life, but in His Word, we receive the fulfillment of all His promises, including the promise of eternal life with Him. When praying this verse before reading the Bible, you are acknowledging your need to rely fully on God's *promises* of intervention, redemption, and life as you learn from His Word. It's not about what you take from the Word but about what God and His Word give.

While many of these terms seem better suited for a courtroom or a government agency, they are the words of God's kingdom in Christ Jesus. They are the words of life in this world and in the new creation to come. Psalm 119 repeatedly portrays God giving life, education, enlightenment, growth, and salvation through His Word. Like in the Lord's Prayer, each petition or request in Psalm 119 serves also as a confession of our need and an acknowledgment that only the Lord through His Word can meet our need. This brings us back to the importance of listening as the Lord speaks to us through His Word.

When you prepare to read the Bible, start by reading a stanza of Psalm 119. The stanzas' alphabetical arrangement provides a sequence of prayers to use each time—a little prayer book. Pay close attention as you pray the psalm, and you will see those words being answered as you read the

Bible. The psalm's words of God will echo in the other words of God you read. Your thoughts will be drawn to the words of praise, thanksgiving, and petition to the Lord for what He has done through His Word. Then, each time you finish the psalm, beginning it again will enhance your appreciation of your need and our Lord's rich supply. He always supplies exactly what we need. Amen.

Key Points

- We need to have the noise of our sinful nature turned down so that we can hear the Word of God.

- You can pray God's given prayer about the word of God in Psalm 119, so that the Holy Spirit might suppress your sinful nature and open your heart to hear as you read the Bible.

- Praying the stanzas of Psalm 119 before you read the Bible can help you focus on what God's Word has to say about itself.

Discussion Questions

1. What noises of daily life tend to interfere with listening to the Bible at home? . . . at church? . . . at work?

2. What sort of sinful nature noises interfere with your attempts to listen to the Bible at home? . . . at church? . . . at work?

3. How would praying one of the twenty-two stanzas of Psalm 119 help you listen to the Bible at home? . . . at church? . . . at work?

Action Steps

1. Read Psalm 119:1–8, 168–76.

   a. What words in these verses refer to God's Word?

   b. What are you saying about God's Word as you pray these verses?

2. Think about what each stanza prays for.

   a. What is the same?

   b. What is different?

   c. Does this speak of a need in your life?

Most people read only a small selection from the Bible at a time: a chapter, an event (e.g., the flood), a parable, or the like. Reading a larger portion of the Bible enables you to see the details of the lives of God's people, His intervention, and His interaction with them. You see the various relationships, actions, and events all at work in what you have read. It can be difficult at times to sort them out so that you can take in the fullness of what the Lord is saying and showing you in His Word.

Martin Luther's friend asked him for advice on how to pray. Luther responded in a letter titled "A Simple Way To Pray." In this letter, Luther shared how he reflected on some particular portion of the catechism or single verse of Scripture by making a prayer wreath of four strands out of it.

First, instruction: I read each commandment
and consider what it is teaching me, as intended
by the commandment, and think about what
God is so earnestly demanding of me.

Second, thanksgiving: I use the commandment
to thank God for something.

Third, confession of sin.

Fourth, I use the commandment to say a prayer using
these or similar words. (Luther, *A Simple Way to Pray*, 16)

Using this process, Luther understood the words he was reading to be eternal and living truths that God had chosen for him to know and by which God would change him. The sequence Luther chose shows that every encounter with the Word of God is first a receiving of what is not known and a revelation to the reader/hearer. Second, it is the receiver's immediate response of gratitude for the Lord having revealed Himself. Third, it is a humble acknowledgement of one's sinful self in light of God's revelation. Fourth, it's a selfless way forward in living the faith by acknowledging one's need for the Lord's intercession on our behalf and requesting to be given all that is needful.

You can also use Luther's process when reading a larger section of the Bible. When reading, note a verse or two that caught your attention. When you are done reading, go back to those verses and apply Luther's four strands.

Each of the four parts in Luther's process testifies to the true sequence of faith where the reader is always (1) a receiver from God and (2) a responder to God. This echoes the very pattern of creation: God spoke, and even the void responded. Genesis 1 and 2 shows the blessed succession of God speaking and creation responding. The order of worship follows in this same pattern of God speaking and the Church, as God's new creation, responding. Luther's process continues this pattern for those who have been re-created in Christ. The Lord continues to speak, and we, as His new creation, respond. Each part in Luther's process aids readers in a more faithful response to the Lord according to what they have just read in His Word.

What follows is an expanded form of Luther's four strands. Under each strand is a series of questions you can ask. The goal is to apply this to the section(s) of the Bible you have read so you may better respond in prayer. These questions are designed to help you search through the text. As the Holy Spirit leads you to consider the questions, the answers you discover will serve as the basis of your prayer.

Depending on how you read, it is helpful to apply the four strands to an individual section of the Bible. While you may read an entire chapter, it would be more beneficial to apply the four strands to one section at a time. This allows you to fully hear what the Lord is saying on each topic and respond accordingly.

Under each of the strands is a simple question, though it may at times seem hard to apply to what you've read. Therefore, after each initial question is a series of sub-questions that can help narrow your focus. It is important to remember there may not be answers to all of the sub-questions, so please do not feel like you have to find an answer for each one.

1. Instruction

What is God teaching me *(and what have I learned)* . . .

. . . *about Himself—Father, Son, and Holy Spirit—as the Trinity?*

. . . *about God's thoughts, words, and deeds?*

. . . *about the thoughts, words, and deeds of those in the text?*

. . . about me and/or others?

. . . about my thoughts, words, and deeds?

. . . about sin and grace?

. . . about life and death, living and dying?

. . . about faith and doubt, belief and unbelief?

. . . about this world and the next?

While you ponder these questions and the ones below, you might want to write down your answers, along with a note on the section of the Bible you have read. For this first strand, your header might begin with *"God is teaching me . . ."* As you write each of these down, you could list the verse in which you found what He taught you. Some of your answers may be painful to acknowledge, let alone write down. But acknowledging them will allow you to bring them to the Lord in confession so that you can be cleansed through Christ's purifying forgiveness.

2. Thanksgiving

What have I learned in this text for which I should give thanks to God?

What is God—the Father, Son, and Holy Spirit—for me?

What has God—the Father, Son, and Holy Spirit—done for me?

What spiritual or earthly blessings did I receive?

What understanding did I receive?

What good news did I hear?

What encouragement/hope did I receive?

3. Confession of Sin

Have all my thoughts, words, and actions been faithful
to what God has said to me in the text?

What have I done that is contrary to what God has said?

What have I failed to do according to what God has said?

As you ponder these questions or others in light of what
you have read, it would serve you well to also write down
answers. For this third strand, you will have two headers. The
first might begin with "*I have sinned against God by . . .*" and
the second header could begin with "*I have sinned against
God by not . . .*"

4. Prayer

What is God's will for me according to what I have read?

What would God have me start or continue to think, say, or do?

*What would God have me stop or continue to refrain
from thinking, saying, or doing?*

Putting the Word to Prayer

Having meditated upon what you have read and having
answered the questions as the Holy Spirit led you, you are
now ready to turn your reading and study of the Word into
prayer. Your answers to the questions become the basis of
your prayer. Use the following opening words to complete
your prayer based upon the text you have read.

1. INSTRUCTION

*Heavenly Father, in what Your Word has taught me, I have come
to know that . . .*

Tell the Lord what you have learned through your study
of His Word. Pray for yourself according to what you have
learned; pray for your family and/or your congregation.

2. THANKSGIVING

*Gracious and giving Lord, in what Your Word has taught me,
I thank You for . . .*

Give thanks to the Lord for what you have written. Give
thanks for what the Lord has done for you, your family, and/
or your congregation.

3. CONFESSION OF SIN

*Merciful and forgiving Lord, in light of what Your Word
has taught me, I confess to You that . . .*

Prayerfully repent and ask His forgiveness for the sake
of Christ. Confess your sins, and ask God's forgiveness for
yourself, your family, and/or your congregation.

4. PRAYER

*Holy Spirit and Guide, in light of what Your Word has taught
me, grant . . .*

Prayerfully ask God to grant you to do His will. Ask God
to grant these same things for your family and/or your congregation.

Putting the Word to Prayer

In this way, your responses to the questions are turned into prayers. While the prayers would first be for yourself, as the one who has heard the Word of God, you can go back over your list and pray for these same things for your family and/or your church. As no one is able to confess the personal sins of another, you would not offer a confession for your family or congregation. What follows are examples of both types of prayer for the first, second, and fourth strands, as well as a prayer for yourself using the third strand, confession of sin.

PSALM 23

Using the questions under each strand, read Psalm 23. As mentioned before, note that not every sub-question is answered. That's fine. Find relevant answers when possible and don't be afraid to challenge yourself; however, don't force an answer when none is apparent to you.

1. Instruction

What is God teaching me? *(What have I learned?)*

. . . about Himself—Father, Son, Holy Spirit—as the Trinity?

He is my shepherd. He makes me lie down in green pastures. He leads me beside still waters. He restores my soul. He leads me in paths of righteousness. He is with me. His rod and staff comfort me. He prepares a table for me in the presence of my enemies. He anoints my head with oil.

. . . about God's thoughts, words, and deeds?

> He is involved with my life. He does things for me.
> He does things to me.

. . . about the thoughts, words, and deeds of those in the text?
. . . about me and/or others?

> I am provided for by the Lord.
>
> I am laid down to rest, I am led, I am restored, I am
> companioned, I am comforted, I have a table
> prepared for me, and I am anointed—by the Lord.
> I am walking through the valley of the shadow
> of death. My cup overflows. Goodness and mercy
> shall follow me all the days of my life. I shall
> dwell in the house of the Lord forever.

. . . about my thoughts, words, and deeds?
. . . about sin and grace?
. . . about life and death, living and dying?

> Even though I'm surrounded by death, it is nothing to fear.

. . . about faith and doubt, belief and unbelief?
. . . about this world and the next?

> God preserves and protects us in this world, though
> there are dangers and enemies around us. He pre-
> pares a place in His house for us to dwell forever.

PUTTING IT ALL TO PRAYER

(FOR SELF) Heavenly Father, in what Your Word has taught me, I have come to know that You are my Shepherd who gives me rest, leads me in peace, restores my soul, leads me in the ways that are right, is with me always, comforts me, provides for me even when my enemies want to take everything from me, and anoints my head with oil. In all this, I have learned how much You are actively involved in my life. I have learned that You do all this because of Your goodness and mercy so that I might dwell with You forever. In Jesus' name. Amen.

(FOR FAMILY) Heavenly Father, in what Your Word has taught me, I have come to know that You are my family's Shepherd and that You give them rest, lead them in peace, restore their souls, lead them in the ways that are right, are with them always, comfort them, provide for them even when their enemies want to take everything from them, and anoint their heads with oil. In all this, I have learned how much You are actively involved in their lives. I have learned that You do all this because of Your goodness and mercy so that they might dwell with You forever. In Jesus' name. Amen.

2. Thanksgiving

What have I learned in this text for which I should give thanks to God?

What is God—the Father, Son, and Holy Spirit—for me?

He is my Shepherd.

What has God—the Father, Son, and Holy Spirit—done for me?

He makes me lie down in green pastures. He leads me
beside still waters. He restores my soul. He leads me
in paths of righteousness. He is with me. His rod and
staff comfort me. He prepares a table for me in the
presence of my enemies. He anoints my head with oil.

What spiritual or earthly blessings did I receive?

Food and water, rest and restoration, comfort, righteousness,
protection

What understanding did I receive?

Though it is humbling, I understand that I am like a sheep.
I understand that the Lord is my shepherd. I understand that as a sheep, I need a shepherd and what He
provides. I understand that no matter how dark things
may be, the Lord is with me. I understand that the Lord
is providing everything for this life so that I may dwell
in His house forever.

What good news did I hear?

The Lord is with me to take care of me.

What encouragement/hope did I receive?

No matter what, the Lord will provide me what I need
for this life and life in heaven.

PUTTING IT ALL TO PRAYER

(FOR SELF) Gracious and giving Lord, in what Your Word has taught me, I thank You for being my Shepherd and doing all that a shepherd does to protect and provide for his sheep. I thank You for continuing to lead and restore me. I thank You for always being with me wherever I am, in all circumstances, to protect and comfort me. I thank You that my cup overflows with more than I need for this life. I thank You for anointing me as Your own for this life and for life in heaven. I thank You for Your goodness and mercy that You send for my welfare in this life and the next. In Jesus' name. Amen.

(FOR FAMILY) Gracious and giving Lord, in what Your Word has taught me, I thank You for being my family's Shepherd and doing all that a shepherd does to protect and provide for his sheep. I thank You for continuing to lead and restore them. I thank You for always being with them wherever they are, in all circumstances, to protect and comfort them. I thank You that their cups overflows with more than they need for this life. I thank You for anointing them as Your own for this life and for life in heaven. I thank You for Your goodness and mercy that You send after them for their welfare in this life and the next. In Jesus' name. Amen.

3. Confession of Sin

Have all my thoughts, words, and actions been faithful to what God has said to me in the text?

What have I done that is contrary to what God has said?

I tend to see my wants as unmet needs and doubt what the Lord provides. I tend to fear the evil more than I trust that the Lord is with me. I tend to selfishly see my cup as empty rather than overflowing.

What have I failed to do according to what God has said?

I haven't followed my Lord and Shepherd as I ought. I haven't trusted Him to provide all I need and protect me.

PUTTING IT ALL TO PRAYER

(FOR SELF) Merciful and forgiving Lord, in light of what Your Word has taught me, I confess to You that I have doubted that what You provide meets my needs. I confess that I have not followed everywhere You led me through Your Word. I confess that I have feared other people or losing earthly things more than losing You. I confess that I have judged my cup to be empty because I don't have all the earthly things I want. I confess that I have not followed You, my Shepherd, or trusted You fully for provision and protection. Be merciful to me for the sake of Jesus Christ, and forgive all my sins and all that I am. In Jesus' name. Amen.

4. Prayer

What is God's will for me according to what I have read?

What would God have me start or continue to think, say, or do?

God wants me to continue to believe and trust in the Lord as my shepherd; to see all that He provides and does for me; to follow His leading, especially through His Word;

to fear no evil; to receive His comfort; to trust in His anointing of me in Baptism; to give thanks for all that flows in and over my cup; to give thanks for the goodness and mercy the Lord sends after me all the days of my life; and to always stay in the house of the Lord, the Church here on earth, so that I might dwell in it in eternity.

What would God have me stop or continue to refrain from thinking, saying, or doing?

God would have me stop focusing on my selfish desires and stop fearing my enemies, even death.

PUTTING IT ALL TO PRAYER

(FOR SELF) Holy Spirit and Guide, in light of what Your Word has taught me, grant me to continue to believe and trust in the Lord as my Shepherd. Grant that I may rightly see all that He does for me to meet my needs. Grant that I may follow Him in His Word so that I fear no evil, receive His comfort, and trust in His anointing in my Baptism. Grant that I may be grateful and filled with praise for all that the Lord causes to fill and overflow my cup. Grant that I may seek the Lord's goodness and mercy, so that I may dwell in His house all the days of my life now and in eternity. In Jesus' name. Amen.

(FOR FAMILY) Holy Spirit and Guide, in light of what Your Word has taught me, grant my family to continue to believe and trust in the Lord as their Shepherd. Grant that they may

rightly see all that He does for them to meet their needs. Grant that they may follow Him in His Word so that they fear no evil, receive His comfort and trust in His anointing in their Baptism. Grant that they may be grateful and filled with praise for all that the Lord causes to fill and overflow their cups. Grant that they may seek the Lord's goodness and mercy so that they may dwell in His house all the days of their lives now and in eternity. In Jesus' name. Amen.

The answers to the questions and the prayers you come up with may well differ from what is offered here. These give you a glimpse at just some of the things you can discover and pray about as you read the Bible prayerfully.

Key Points

- Luther used a process to reflect on what he was reading in the Bible called the four strands.

- Each part of Luther's process focuses the reader on the sequence of faith, first receiving from God, then responding to God.

- Each part of the process aides readers in a more faithful response according to what has just been read.

Discussion Questions

1. When reading a whole chapter of the Bible or a section of the Bible, do you find it difficult to notice the details? How do you see this process helping you?

2. When reading whole sections of the Bible, do you find it difficult to apply them to yourself? How do you see this process helping you?

3. How can this process help you to turn what you read into prayer? Why is praying about the specific readings you're encountering in Scripture so beneficial?

Action Steps

Read Genesis 18:22–33.

● Look over the whole section of the Bible to hear the details of what you read.

● Apply the questions based on Luther's four strands to what you have read and write down the answers.

● Turn your answers to the four strands into prayers for yourself, your family, and/or your church.

Apply the Four Strands

Using your answers from above, continue your study by answering the questions for the four strands.

FIRST STRAND—INSTRUCTION

What is God teaching me *(and what have I learned)* . . .

. . . about Himself—Father, Son, and Holy Spirit—as the Trinity?

. . . about God's thoughts, words, and deeds?

. . . about the thoughts, words, and deeds of those in the text?

. . . about me and/or others?

. . . about my thoughts, words, and deeds?

. . . about sin and grace?

. . . about life and death, living and dying?

. . . about faith and doubt, belief and unbelief?

. . . about this world and the next?

SECOND STRAND—THANKSGIVING

What have I learned in this text for which I should give thanks to God?

What is God—the Father, Son, and Holy Spirit—for me?

What has God—the Father, Son, and Holy Spirit—done for me?

What spiritual or earthly blessings did I receive?

What understanding did I receive?

What good news did I hear?

What encouragement/hope did I receive?

THIRD STRAND—CONFESSION OF SIN

Have all my thoughts, words, and actions been faithful to what God has said to me in the text?

What have I done that is contrary to what God has said?

What have I failed to do according to what God has said?

FOURTH STRAND—PRAYER

What is God's will for me according to what I have read?

What would God have me start or continue to think, say, or do?

What would God have me stop or continue to refrain from thinking, saying, or doing?

Putting the Word to Prayer

Using your answers from the four strands, draft your prayers below.

FIRST—INSTRUCTION

Heavenly Father, in what Your Word has taught me, I have come to know that . . .

SECOND—THANKSGIVING

Gracious and giving Lord, in what Your Word has taught me, I thank You for . . .

THIRD—CONFESSION OF SIN

Merciful and forgiving Lord, in light of what Your Word has taught me, I confess to You that . . .

FOURTH—PRAYER

Holy Spirit and Guide, in light of what Your Word has taught me, grant . . .

Now you can apply this to any section of the Bible you read.

After reading a section of the Bible, go back through to find one verse that stands out. Examine this verse alone to see more closely what the Lord is saying to you and respond accordingly in prayer.

Having learned how we may take in the beauty of hills and valleys (i.e., a section of Scripture), we now move on to the individual trees (i.e., specific verses). Luther's "A Simple Way to Pray" was designed to help take the beauty of the individual verse and turn it into prayer. As each tree has many different leaves, so each verse has many different words. Each word, like each leaf on a tree, has unique beauty in itself that adds beauty to the whole.

In the words of a particular verse, we are looking for three different types: *verb*, *subject*, and *direct object*. These are essential for any real verbal communication to take place. Every pastor is trained to look for these three types of words when they learn Greek and Hebrew. An understanding of the purpose and relationship between these words is critical if a pastor is going to faithfully translate and interpret the biblical languages. When you read the Bible, do you think about the sentences you read, their structure and relationship to one another? While it sounds mundane, the function of words and their relationship to one another is critical to hearing and understanding what you read.

The First Word: Verbs

Because the verb is the heart of every sentence, it needs to be found first. Without the verb, there can be little real communication. Verbs are used primarily in two ways. The first and most common way a verb is used is to show action.

> "Whoever *receives* you *receives* Me, and whoever *receives* Me *receives* Him who sent Me." (Matthew 10:40, emphasis added)

Here the verb "receives" is used to show the type of action "whoever" is doing. The other way a verb is used is to show the state or condition of a person, place, thing, or idea.

> "For the Son of Man *is* lord of the Sabbath." (Matthew 12:8, emphasis added)

Here the verb "is" is used to show the state of the "Son of Man," which is that He "is lord of the Sabbath."

Verbs do more than merely show action or the state of something; they also put static objects into motion. As verbs show the state or condition of something, they also clarify and differentiate persons, places, things, or ideas. Verbs are the heart of communication because they show the relationship between things. Let's use the verses above to illustrate.

> "Whoever receives you receives Me, and whoever receives Me receives Him who sent Me."

While the verb "receives" shows the action of receiving,

it also shows the relational movement of "you" to "whoever." Without the action shown through the verb, the subject (whoever) and the direct object (you) would remain static, apart from one another and without any relationship. The verb brings "you" and "whoever" into a relationship, making "you" the giver and "whoever" the receiver.

"For the Son of Man is lord of the Sabbath."

While the verb "is" shows that the state of the "Son of Man" is that of "lord of the Sabbath," it also differentiates the "Son of Man" from all others as "lord of the Sabbath."

In addition, verbs show whether the action or state of being was in the past, the present, or the future. These tenses can fill verbs with much comfort for the reader. Consider how a change of tense would affect the comfort found in Jesus' words "It is finished" (John 19:30). Here the verb "finish" is in the past tense, "finished," and shows that the wrath of God against all our sin has been fully suffered to the point that there is none left. If we change the tense of the verb to present, it reads, "It is finishing." This would mean that the full wrath of God has not yet been fully expressed, it is not done, there is more of it yet to come, and, while it will be finished at some point, we can never know when.

In Greek, the present tense is often used to convey more than something taking place now. Present tense is often used to show action or state of being that is to be continuous. In Mark 1:14–15 we read, "Now after John was arrested, Jesus came into Galilee, proclaiming the gospel of God, and saying, 'The time is fulfilled, and the kingdom of God is at hand; repent and believe in the gospel.' " The verbs "repent" and "believe" in the Greek are both present tense; they are imperatives, commands to do something. In the Greek, this means that Jesus' words are heard as "the kingdom of God is at hand, *be always repenting* and *be always believing* in the gospel." It is not written this way in the English because putting in all implied understandings of the Greek into the English would make it almost impossible to read. So when examining the verbs, the tense can carry more meaning than the literal translation from the Greek to English. Listening for this can bring great comfort.

When the verb is cast in the future tense, usually preceded by the words *will* or *shall*, it sets before the reader something that shall take place in the future. When the Lord speaks using the future tense, He gives rise to the uniqueness of Christian hope over human hope. Jesus speaks of the future in John 14:3–4: "And if I go and prepare a place for you, I will come again and will take you to Myself, that where I am you may be also." The verbs "come" and "take" are preceded by the word "will," indicating the specific promise Jesus makes of what He will do without exception. This gives absolute certainty to what He will do, and this gives the Christian the certainty of what will happen. Again, the future tense in the Word of God speaks of what shall happen no matter what. Jesus expresses this reality in John 11:25–26: "I am the resurrection and the life. Whoever believes in Me, though he die, yet shall he live, and everyone who lives and believes in Me shall never die." Although a believer dies, it cannot keep him or her from living, because Christ is the resurrection and the life. This stands in stark contrast to mere human hope for the future, which is built upon what will happen as long as nothing interferes with it. The future tense brings much comfort in the Word of God.

The Second Word: Subject

The subject of the sentence needs the verb, and the verb needs the subject to show who is doing the action or to whom the state of being belongs. To identify the subject's purpose in communication, consider one of the best-known and best-loved verses of the Bible: "For God so loved the world, that He gave His only Son, that whoever believes in Him should not perish but have eternal life" (John 3:16). In the first phrase, the verb is "loved." Who is doing this action of loving? The answer is "God," who is the subject of the sentence. The subject is usually right before the verb in the sentence structure. By identifying the subject of the verb, the reader is better able to know whether the verse is Law or Gospel. If the doer of the verb is human, it will tend to be Law. If God the Father, Son, or Holy Spirit is the doer, this tends to be the Gospel. If the subject of the verse is God, the sentence likely provides the basis of faith. When God is the doer, the reader is given the power to believe in and live by what the sentence says about Him and His actions.

The Third Word: The Direct Object

The third basic word type found in most sentences is the direct object. This word is also found in this first part of John 3:16: "For God so loved the world." To find the direct object, we return to the verb "loved," this time asking not who is doing the love, but who is receiving the love. The direct object shows the receiver of the action and is usually found right after the verb. In this text, "the world" is the direct object because it is the receiver of God's action of love.

The verb/action:	*loved*
The subject/doer:	*God*
The direct object/receiver:	*the world*

Consider the second phrase of John 3:16: "that He gave His only Son." To find the verb, subject, and direct object, we will ask three simple questions. (1) Which word shows the action or state of being (verb)? (2) Which word shows the doer (subject)? (3) And which word shows the receiver of the action (direct object)?

What is the action/verb?	*gave*
Who is doing the giving?	*God*
Who is receiving the giving?	*the world*

Here the direct object, the receiver of God's giving, is not found. When this happens, the reader needs to return to the first or last phrase of the sentence to find the direct object (receiver) of the giving. In this verse, the receiver of the action is found in the first clause. Just as "the world" was the receiver of God's love, so in the second clause, "the world" is understood as the receiver of what God gave, namely His only Son.

Let's examine the last clause of the sentence: "that whoever believes in Him should not perish but have eternal life." Again, we ask the same three questions. (1) Which words are used to show the action or state of being? (2) Which word is used to show the doer? (3) And which word is used to show the receiver of the action? (Note that this last part of the verse has two verbs, so we will want to find the main or key verb.)

What is the first action/verb?	**believes** (main verb because the next verb is dependent upon it)
What is the second action/verb?	**perish** (secondary because it is a result of the first verb)
Who is doing the believing?	**whoever**
Who is not doing the perishing?	**whoever believes**
Who is receiving the believing?	**Him** (God's Son that He gave)

Having asked these questions about the three clauses in John 3:16, what information did we harvest?

First Clause:	**For God so loved the world,**
Verb:	**loved**
Subject:	**God**
Direct Object:	**the world**

Second Clause:	*that He gave His only Son,*
Verb:	*gave*
Subject:	*He*
Direct Object:	*the world* (implied from first clause)
Third Clause:	*that whoever believes in Him should not perish but have eternal life.*
Verb 1:	*believes*—primary
Subject:	*whoever*
Direct Object:	*Him* (God's Son)—the one God gave.
Verb 2:	*not perish*—secondary
Subject:	*Him* (God's Son)
Direct Object:	*whoever* (believes in God's Son)

When doing your word study, it is important that you study an entire sentence, not just a single verse. The sentence structure is the key to understanding the verb, subject, and direct object, their function and their relationships. You will find that often a single sentence can stretch through multiple verses.

With the information your word study provides, you can go on to ask and answer the same series of questions based on Luther's "A Simple Way to Pray." Asking these questions of a single verse was Luther's original intention. When these are asked of your word study, it yields more wonderful things for you to offer in prayer.

Putting the Word to Prayer

Let's apply the expanded form of Luther's four strands to the word study results for John 3:16 and then put it all to prayer.

1. Instruction

What is God teaching me *(and what have I learned)* . . .

. . . about Himself—Father, Son, Holy Spirit—as the Trinity?

He is loving. He is giving.

. . . about God's thoughts, words, and deeds?

He loves the world; this means He loves me and everyone in the world. The Father sacrificed His only Son so that whoever believes in His Son will not perish but have eternal life.

. . . about the thoughts, words, and deeds of those in the text?

. . . about me and/or others?

As a part of the world, every person is loved by God. God gave His Son to me and everyone else. By the power of the Holy Spirit, everyone can believe in God's Son. Without faith, I and everyone else would perish. Without faith, neither I nor anyone else can have eternal life.

. . . about my thoughts, words, and deeds?

. . . about sin and grace?

Grace: God gave His Son to save me from perishing in hell.
I receive His Son through God's gift of faith.

Sin: The fact that everyone without faith in God's Son
perishes shows that sin is powerful and destructive.
The fact that God gives eternal life only through faith
in His Son means that apart from faith no one has
or can have eternal life.

. . . about life and death, living and dying?

No one has to perish eternally, because God offers eternal
life to all who believe.

. . . about faith and doubt, belief and unbelief?

Through faith in God's Son, no one will perish but have
eternal life. Faith in Him has everlasting consequences
—both in its presence and its absence.

. . . about this world and the next?

The world (all people) is loved by God. God wants to save
the world. The world has been given God's Son. The
world is perishing and does not have eternal life.

PUTTING IT ALL TO PRAYER

(FOR SELF) Heavenly Father, in what Your Word has
taught me, I have come to know that You are loving and You
are giving. You love everyone in the world and want to save
everyone. Without faith in Your Son, everyone will perish and
never have eternal life. But You love us so much that You

have given Your Son, so that whoever believes in Him will not perish but have eternal life. You do all of this because You love everyone and want all to be saved. This means that Your love and want for me is eternal. In Jesus' name. Amen.

(FOR FAMILY) Heavenly Father, in what Your Word has taught me, I have come to know that You are loving and You are giving. You have loved my family and want to save my family. Without faith in Your Son, my family will perish and never have eternal life. But You love my family so much that You have given Your Son, so that if my family believes in Him, they will not perish but have eternal life. You do all this for my family because You love everyone and want all to be saved. This means that Your love and want for my family is eternal. In Jesus' name. Amen.

2. Thanksgiving

What have I learned in this text for which I should give thanks to God?

What is God—the Father, Son, and Holy Spirit—for me?
He is loving. He is personally giving to and for me.

What has God—the Father, Son, and Holy Spirit—done for me?
He loves me. He gave His Son to save me and gives me eternal life through faith in Him.

What spiritual or earthly blessings did I receive?
I will not perish if I believe in His Son. He gives me eternal life through faith in His Son.

What understanding did I receive?

God's love alone is the reason He gave His Son to save me and all people. This makes my salvation about His love, not about what I have done. This means that God wants me for His own reasons.

What good news did I hear?

God loves me and wants me so much that He gave His Son to save me. My sense of worth doesn't depend on me or the judgment of the world.

What encouragement/hope did I receive?

No matter what others think of me or do to me, I am loved and wanted by God in this life and the life to come. Because of God's love in giving me His Son, I will live eternally.

PUTTING IT ALL TO PRAYER

(FOR SELF) Gracious and giving Lord, in what Your Word has taught me, I thank You for being so loving and wanting of me and all people that You gave Your only Son, so that through faith in Him no one will perish but have eternal life. I thank You that Your eternal love for me comes from You and not from anything I have done or could ever do. Thank You for letting me hear this good and saving news. In Jesus' name. Amen.

(FOR FAMILY) Gracious and giving Lord, in what Your Word has taught me, I thank You for being so loving and want-

ing of my family that You gave Your only Son, so that through faith in Him none of them will perish but have eternal life. I thank You that Your eternal love for my family comes from You and not from anything they have done or could ever do. Thank You for letting my family hear this good and saving news. In Jesus' name. Amen.

3. Confession of Sin

Have all my thoughts, words, and actions been faithful to what God has said to me in the text?

What have I done that is contrary to what God has said?
I have questioned whether He really loves me.
I have questioned whether He really wants me.
I have questioned whether He should love and want others.

What have I failed to do according to what God has said?
I have failed to always believe in His love and His Son.
I have not always believed that He actually loves and wants others just as much as He loves and wants me.

PUTTING IT ALL TO PRAYER

(FOR SELF) Merciful and forgiving Lord, in light of what Your Word has taught me, I confess to You that I have questioned whether You really love me and want me to be saved, and I have looked elsewhere for love. I have questioned whether others deserve Your love or Your desire to save them

when I think they are undeserving. I have not always believed in Your love and want of me and others. Lord, have mercy on me and forgive me these and all my sins for the sake of Your Son, Jesus Christ. Amen.

4. Prayer

What is God's will for me according to what I have read?

What would God have me start or continue to think, say, or do?

He wants me to always believe in His love and the gift of His Son. I should be forever grateful for His love, want, and gift to me in His Son. God wants me to always believe that His love and gift are for all people so that I share His love and His Son with everyone.

What would God have me stop or continue to refrain from thinking, saying, or doing?

He wants me to stop questioning His love and want of me in His Son. I should stop questioning His love and want for everyone else. I should stop rationing how much I share His love and want for others and the gift of His Son.

PUTTING IT ALL TO PRAYER

(FOR SELF) Holy Spirit and Guide, in light of what Your Word has taught me, grant that I may always believe in God's love and want for me in His Son. Grant that I may be ever thankful for His love, want, and gift in His Son. Grant that I may not question His love and want for me or any other per-

son. Grant that I may more and more share with others His love and want for them. In Jesus' name. Amen.

(FOR FAMILY) Holy Spirit and Guide, in light of what Your Word has taught me, grant that my family may always believe in God's love and want for them in His Son. Grant that they may be ever thankful for His love, want, and gift in His Son. Grant that my family may not question His love and want for them or any other person. Grant that my family may more and more share His love and want for others. In Jesus' name. Amen.

Key Points

● Verbs are used primarily in two ways. The most common way a verb is used is to show action. The other way a verb is used is to show the state or condition of a person, place, thing, or idea.

● The purpose of the subject is to communicate who is doing the action or to whom the state of being belongs.

● Identifying the direct object in a sentence indicates the receiver of the action, and it is usually found right after the verb.

Discussion Questions

1. When looking at a particular verse of the Bible, do you normally examine it in terms of what's being done, who's doing it, or for whom it's being done?

2. How do you see this word study process helping you notice these details?

3. What do you see as the benefits of examining a verse in this way?

4. How do you see this word study helping you to turn what you read into prayer?

Action Steps

Read Ephesians 3:20–21.

● Examine the words of the verse, identifying first the *verb* (*action or state of being*), second the *subject* (*doer of the action*), and third the *direct object* (*receiver of the action*), .

● Apply the questions based on Luther's four strands to better understand what the types of words are and what their relationship to each other tells you.

● Turn your answers to the four strands into prayers for yourself, your family, and/or your church.

Word Study

Use the sentence found in Ephesians 3:20–21 to answer the following questions.

1. How many clauses or parts are there to the passage?

2. Find the verbs within the passage. What action or state of being is shown?

What kind of action does the verb show?

What kind of state of being or condition do the verbs show?

Is the action in the past, the present, or the future?

Which verb is the primary or main verb?

3. Find the subject of the verb. Who is the doer of the action?

4. Find the direct object. Who is the receiver of the action?

Apply the Four Strands

Using your answers from above, continue your study by answering the questions for the four strands.

FIRST STRAND—INSTRUCTION

What is God teaching me *(and what have I learned)* . . .

. . . *about Himself—Father, Son, Holy Spirit—as the Trinity?*

. . . *about God's thoughts, words, and deeds?*

. . . *about the thoughts, words, and deeds of those in the text?*

. . . *about me and/or others?*

. . . *about my thoughts, words, and deeds?*

. . . *about sin and grace?*

. . . *about life and death, living and dying?*

. . . *about faith and doubt, belief and unbelief?*

. . . *about this world and the next?*

SECOND STRAND—THANKSGIVING

What have I learned in this text for which I should give thanks to God?

What is God—the Father, Son, and Holy Spirit—for me?

What has God—the Father, Son, Holy Spirit—done for me?

What spiritual or earthly blessings did I receive?

What understanding did I receive?

What good news did I hear?

What encouragement/hope did I receive?

THIRD STRAND—CONFESSION OF SIN

Have all my thoughts, words, and actions been faithful to what God has said to me in the text?

What have I done that is contrary to what God has said?

What have I failed to do according to what God has said?

FOURTH STRAND—PRAYER

What is God's will for me according to what I have read?

What would God have me start or continue to think, say, or do?

What would God have me stop or continue to refrain from thinking, saying, or doing?

Putting the Word to Prayer

Using your answers from the expanded form of the four strands, and if you'd like, your word study, draft your prayers below.

FIRST—INSTRUCTION

Heavenly Father, in what Your Word has taught me, I have come to know that . . .

SECOND—THANKSGIVING

Gracious and giving Lord, in what Your Word has taught me, I thank You for . . .

THIRD—CONFESSION OF SIN

Merciful and forgiving Lord, in light of what Your Word has taught me, I confess to You that . . .

FOURTH—PRAYER

Holy Spirit and Guide, in light of what Your Word has taught me, grant . . .

Among other things, the Bible is a book of promises, going all the way back to two significant promises early in Genesis. The first Gospel promise is of the seed of the woman crushing the head of the serpent (3:15). This is recognized as the Gospel promise of the Savior who would come in human flesh, born of a woman, to save all those born of woman. The first Law promise God made was one of death if Adam and Eve ate of the tree He forbade them to eat (3:3). In these promises are the two great teachings that fill the Bible: Law and Gospel. Both promises are made by God to every human being throughout time. How do we hear and listen to these promises made to us?

John the Baptist helps us hear them in their right relationship: "For the law was given through Moses; grace and truth came through Jesus Christ" (John 1:17). The Law is the will of God for all humanity and the promise of God to all those who reject His will. For God to be true to Himself as God and faithful to His creation, He must be true to His Word. So that His promises may be trusted, they must be kept; God must fulfill His promise of death for all who reject His will—for all who sin. The promise of the Law is always conditional on what you do or fail to do: "If you . . . then I . . ." The truth of the Law, like God who gave it, is unyielding and uncompromising in its conditional demands. There are no points for effort, no curve because of ignorance or weakness. The demands and promises of the Law must be kept by both the Giver and the receiver. Adam and Eve's attempt to hide from God in their shame shows that the Law's promise of death was the only promise they knew. Although the Law's promise provided the conditions upon which death would come, it did not provide any way for them or us to undo what they had done and escape the promised death. The limits of what the Law can do for any person were illustrated by my pastor one Sunday.

Let's say you're driving your car down the road way too fast and way too carelessly. It isn't long before you lose control, veer off the road, and smash into a tree. You are trapped in the car, now on fire.

Along comes someone who sees your situation and comes down to the car. Seeing you inside, this person proceeds to tell you that if you had handled your car according to the "rules of the road," driven your car according to the speed limit, and used your car the way the manufacturer intended for you to handle it, this would not have happened to you.

Now everything this person is telling you is probably true. But you're still stuck in the burning car! In all the truth this person spoke, neither he nor his words of truth got you out of the car.

This illustration reveals the limits of what the Law can do for any of us, as we are all pinned in sin and bound to the fires of hell. The Law will not free us from sin. God's promise of Law must be kept.

God must, however, be completely true to Himself as God, and "God is love" (1 John 4:8, 16). This means that as the essence of God, love is not some emotional or sentimental attitude, but His existence expressed purely for the benefit and welfare of others. God is entirely about actively being and doing for others. My pastor went on to illustrate the reality of the Gospel:

> Then along comes Jesus, promising to get you out of the car and save you from the fire. Not waiting for you to choose whether you want Him to or not, Jesus gets into the car, pushes you out, and is engulfed in flames.

This is the heart of God's true nature and the basis of the second promise to Adam and Eve and all their children. This is God being the love that He is by doing for us what we cannot do. This is the Gospel, the Good News, that unlike the Law, is not conditional; it's not dependent on anything you or I do. The Gospel is purely the grace of God. The grace of God does for you and me all the things we cannot do to be saved and right with Him.

The Gospel doesn't set aside the demands of God's Law, but it is the Word of God in Jesus meeting and fulfilling the demands of the Law to save us from it. Since we cannot deal with the demands of God's Law, God in love sent His Son into our human flesh to meet the demands of His Law and His wrath for us. Everything God does in Christ to save us is Good News because none of it can be found in us or our abilities. The Gospel is Good News in Jesus Christ meeting us where we are to save us from the Law and change us from death to life through faith in Him.

You will find both Law and Gospel throughout the Bible. You will know it is Law if the subject or doer of the action or state of being is not God but a regular person (you): "You shall love the Lord your God with all your heart and with all your soul and with all your mind" (Matthew 22:37). Here the verb is "love," the subject/doer is "you," and the direct object/receiver is "the Lord your God." This verse is Law because it shows or tells the hearer/reader what he must do.

In *Luther's Small Catechism with Explanation*, we learn a simple difference between the Law and the Gospel.

What is the difference between the Law and the Gospel?

A. The Law teaches what we are to do and not to do; the Gospel teaches what God has done, and still does, for our salvation.

B. The Law shows us our sin and the wrath of God; the Gospel shows us our Savior and the grace of God.

C. The Law must be proclaimed to all people, but especially to impenitent sinners; the Gospel

must be proclaimed to sinners who are troubled
in their minds because of their sins. (p. 101)

If what you have read is Law, it will be worded as something you are to do or a judgment on what is not right with
God—sin. At first the Law may seem to be primarily a guide
to godly living, but the moment it is read or heard, an almost automatic self-examination takes place within us. Have
I done this? Did I do that? Am I like that? This begins within us
because we are all bound under the Law and sin. In this way
the Law serves as a mirror with which you examine yourself
to see if you have faithfully kept the Law. In this examina-
tion, you need to keep in mind what the Lord says in Romans
3:22–23: "For there is no distinction: for all have sinned and
fall short of the glory of God." This means that no one can
keep the Law according to what it demands. While this may
seem hard to grasp, the keeping of any of God's Law requires
that you keep it perfectly every time, all the time, and do it
only and always with perfect and pure motives.

Thus the Law shows our sins, our falling short, and drives
us to the Gospel, to the work of God in Christ. For only Christ
has met and fulfilled the demands of the Law for us. The Lord
shows this path in Romans 3:24–25: "[all] are justified by His
grace as a gift, through the redemption that is in Christ Jesus,
whom God put forward as a propitiation by His blood, to be
received by faith." The first part of this text is all Law, and
then God speaks the better word of the Gospel. Therefore,
it's critical when you hear the Law and are convicted by it for

not being or doing what is right that you turn in repentance to the better word of the Gospel. Repent and turn to the work of Jesus Christ to justify you by His grace.

If what you are reading is Gospel, the subject or doer of the action or state of being will be God the Father, Jesus Christ, or the Holy Spirit. The Gospel always shows God's attributes and actions involved in saving, preserving, and delivering His people from the power of sin, death, and the devil. The John 3:16 verse we examined previously shows God as the lover of the world and as the giver of His Son to the world. This is pure Gospel. The last clause of John 3:16 shows "whoever" as the one who "believes" in God's Son. This would seem to be Law, but it is in fact Gospel because what is believed is God's act of love and giving, rather than the act of man. In God's act of loving us and giving to us He gives the ability to believe in it. Apart from His giving, you had and can have nothing of the kind in which to believe.

As mentioned before, you may find that the entire section you are reading is completely Law, with not a word of God's saving work to be found in it. When reading such a section, make sure to hear it in the larger context of the whole Bible. The reason for this is that the whole Bible finds its fulfillment in the saving work of Christ alone.

> For the Son of God, Jesus Christ, whom we proclaimed among you, Silvanus and Timothy and I, was not Yes and No, but in Him it is always Yes. For all the promises

of God find their Yes in Him. That is why it is through Him that we utter our Amen to God for His glory. And it is God who establishes us with you in Christ, and has anointed us, and who has also put His seal on us and given us His Spirit in our hearts as a guarantee. (2 Corinthians 1:19–22)

This means that every single demand and promise of the Law upon you finds its yes in Jesus because He met and kept every one of them for you. It further means that every promise of God's mercy, love, and saving grace finds their yes in Jesus for you.

Just as you may find that an entire section of what you read is Law, you may also read a section or verse that is all Gospel. Not a word telling you what to do, showing your sin, or condemning you for what you have done in sin. So how do you hear the Law when the reading is purely Gospel? The context in which the verse or section is found will help the reader find the Law. While this does not occur often, there are verses and small sections that are pure Gospel. Where there is pure Gospel, there is with it implied Law. So how do we find it? The key is to remember that the Gospel refers to the merciful and gracious words/works of God done in Jesus Christ for the salvation of all. The Law is covered by the specific Gospel words/works that God has done to save you. Consider Ephesians 2:8–9: "For by grace you have been saved through faith. And this is not your own doing; it is the gift of God, not a result of works, so that no one may boast." These verses are pure Gospel. To find the Law, look at the main verb, "saved." To save something implies that it lacks the ability to save itself and will be lost. We cannot save ourselves from our sin and the verdict of the Law against us.

Finding and listening to these two great words of Law and Gospel is significantly aided by word study and Luther's "A Simple Way To Pray." When you read the Bible, these questions will help you discover whether the text is Law or Gospel.

Hearing the Law and the Gospel

The following questions are offered as a way for you to better hear and distinguish what you are reading as Law or Gospel. Once you have read through these questions, you are ready to turn to the Lord in prayer according to the Law and/or the Gospel you have heard Him speak to you.

IS IT LAW?

In what you've read, . . .

. . . *is there something that shows what I am to do or not do?*

. . . *is there something said about sin?*

. . . *is there something said about sinners (me)?*

. . . *is there something that shows God's punishment of sin and/ or sinners?*

. . . *is there something said or shown about unbelief or lack of faith?*

These questions are not exhaustive, but they will help you know whether this is something done, to be done, or suffered *by* you.

In what you've read, . . .

. . . is there something that shows what God (Father, Son, or Holy Spirit) is doing or giving for the sake of someone?

. . . is there something that shows God's saving work?

. . . is there something that shows God's mercy?

. . . is there something that shows God's undeserved love or work for the sake of someone (grace)?

. . . is there something said or shown about faith?

Again, the questions offered are not exhaustive, but they will serve to help you know whether this is something done, to be done, or suffered *for* you by God.

As you ponder each of these questions, it would serve you well to write down your answers. As you write down your answers under these two headings, you might want to note the verses where you found them. If you would like to ponder further what you've discovered in this study, you can apply the four strands of Luther's "A Simple Way to Pray." For our purposes in this process, you're ready to take what you have learned to the Lord in prayer by using the expanded form of Luther's four strands.

Application: Hearing the Law and the Gospel

Using the questions under *Is It Law?* and *Is It Gospel?* let's examine 2 Corinthians 5:1–5.

IS IT LAW?

In what you've read . . .

. . . is there something that shows what I am to do or not do?

. . . is there something said about sin?

. . . is there something said about sinners (me)?

We live in earthly tents (our bodies), which are temporary dwellings, mortal, which will be destroyed.

We groan because we are burdened in our earthly tent.

We groan, longing to put on our heavenly dwelling that we don't have now.

We are mortal, which means we cannot live forever unless we are swallowed by life.

. . . is there something that shows God's punishment of sin and/ or sinners?

. . . is there something said or shown about unbelief or lack of faith?

IS IT GOSPEL?

In what you've read . . .

. . . is there something that shows what God (Father, Son, or Holy Spirit) is doing or giving for the sake of someone?

He has given us an eternal building He has made in the heavens.

He has prepared us to receive this heavenly home.

He has given us His Spirit as a guarantee.

. . . is there something that shows God's saving work?

He gives us an eternal building so that when our earthly mortal tents are destroyed, we won't be destroyed with them.

He swallows up our mortality with life.

He prepares us for it.

He gives us His Spirit as a guarantee.

. . . is there something that shows God's mercy?

Not directly.

. . . is there something that shows God's undeserved love or work for the sake of someone (grace)?

He gives us an eternal building in heaven.

He swallows up our mortal lives with life.

He prepares us to receive all this.

He gives us His Spirit so that we can have a guarantee that all this would be ours.

. . . is there something said or shown about faith?

No.

Putting the Word to Prayer

Using your answers to the questions, you can now bring them to the Lord in prayer. Complete the opening words of prayer with what you have discovered. Remember that what you turn into prayer for yourself can also be for your family and/or congregation. Again, as no one is able to confess the personal sins of another, we do not offer such a confession for our family or congregation.

INSTRUCTION

(FOR SELF) Heavenly Father, in what Your Word has taught me, I have come to know that my physical body is like an earthly tent; it is temporary and will be destroyed. I have learned that I am burdened in this body and I am mortal; I will die unless You swallow me up with life. I have learned that the groaning that takes place within in me is not all because of my burdens but also because of my eager desire to be rid of my tent and live in the house You have prepared for me. I have learned that You have prepared me to receive an eternal building in heaven when my earthly tent is destroyed. I have learned that You made this building for me and gave me Your Spirit as a guarantee that I shall never be found naked. I have learned that You have swallowed up my mortality by life. I have learned that You have done all this for me because I could never do it for myself. In Jesus' name. Amen.

(FOR FAMILY) Heavenly Father, in what Your Word has taught me, I have come to know that my family's physical

bodies are like earthly tents—they are temporary and will be destroyed. I have learned that they are burdened in their bodies/tents and they are mortal, they will die unless You swallow them up with life. I have learned that the groaning that takes place within them is not all because of their burdens but also because of their eager desire to be rid of their tents and live in the house You have prepared for them. I have learned that You have prepared my family to receive an eternal building in heaven when their earthly tents are destroyed. I have learned that You made this building for them and gave them Your Spirit as a guarantee that they shall never be found naked. I have learned that You have swallowed up their mortality by life. I have learned that You have done all this for my family because they could never do it for themselves. In Jesus' name. Amen.

THANKSGIVING

(FOR SELF) Gracious and giving Lord, in what Your Word has taught me, I thank You for preparing me to receive an eternal building/home in heaven that You have built. I thank You for swallowing up my mortality with life and giving me Your Spirit as a guarantee of this. I thank You that when my tent, my mortal body, dies, You will give me a place in heaven. I thank You for doing all this for me because I can do none of it or be worthy of it. In Jesus' name. Amen.

(FOR FAMILY) Gracious and giving Lord, in what Your Word has taught me, I thank You for preparing my family to receive an eternal building/home in heaven that You have

built. I thank You for swallowing up my family's mortality with life and giving them Your Spirit as a guarantee of this. I thank You that when my family's tents, their mortal bodies, die, You will give them a place in heaven. I thank You for doing all this for my family because they can do none of it or be worthy of it. In Jesus' name. Amen.

CONFESSION OF SIN

(FOR SELF) Merciful and forgiving Lord, in light of what Your Word has taught me, I confess to You that I have lived as if my earthly tent was all that matters. I have not been mindful of my own mortality. I have not sought You and Your preparation in repentance and forgiveness as I ought. Be merciful to me for the sake of Jesus Christ and forgive all my sins and all that I am. In Jesus' name. Amen.

PRAYER

(FOR SELF) Holy Spirit and Guide, in light of what Your Word has taught me, grant that I continue to believe and trust in God's preparation of me and to receive the heavenly building He has built for me. Increase my longing to be clothed with the heavenly dwelling God has for me. Grant that I may give up my mortality to God in repentance and faith so that I may be swallowed up by His life through the forgiveness of my sins. If ever I am led to doubt whether I have God's guarantee of all this, return me to my Baptism, where God gave me You, His Holy Spirit, to wash and rebirth me in eternal life. In Jesus' name. Amen.

(FOR FAMILY) Holy Spirit and Guide, in light of what Your Word has taught me, grant that my family continue to believe and trust in God's preparation of them and to receive the heavenly building He has built for them. Increase their longing to be clothed with the heavenly dwelling God has for them. Grant that my family may give up their mortality to God in repentance and faith so that they may be swallowed up by His life through the forgiveness of their sins. If ever they are led to doubt whether they have God's guarantee of all this, return them to their Baptism where God gave them You, His Holy Spirit, to wash and rebirth them in eternal life. In Jesus' name. Amen.

Key Points

- God speaks two different words to us in the Bible, one Law and the other Gospel.

- Law is what we are to do or not do; the Law shows our sins, our falling short, and drives us to the Gospel, to the work of God in Christ.

- The Gospel is purely the grace and work of God. The Gospel doesn't set aside the demands of God's Law, but it is the Word of God in Jesus meeting, fulfilling, and saving us from the demands of the Law.

Discussion Questions

1. When reading the Bible, how do you tell whether a particular passage is Law or Gospel?

2. How do you see this process helping you distinguish between the two?

3. What do you see as the benefits of examining a text in this way?

4. How do you expect distinguishing between the Law and Gospel to help you turn what you read into prayer?

Action Steps

Read Numbers 14:13–24.

● Identify the Law and/or Gospel in what you have read by asking questions.

● Using Luther's four strands, turn your answers to the Law/Gospel questions into prayer for yourself, your family, and/or your church.

Hearing the Law and the Gospel

Using the following questions, work through Numbers 14:13–24 to see which words are Law and which words are Gospel.

IS IT LAW?

In what you've read . . .

. . . is there something that shows what I am to do or not do?

. . . is there something said about sin?

. . . is there something said about sinners (me)?

. . . *is there something that shows God's punishment of sin and/
or sinners?*

. . . *is there something said or shown about unbelief or lack of
faith?*

These questions are not exhaustive but they will help
you know whether this is something done, to be done, or
suffered *by* you.

IS IT GOSPEL?

In what you've read . . .

. . . *is there something that shows what God, (Father, Son/Jesus,
or Holy Spirit) is doing or giving for the sake of someone?*

. . . *is there something that shows God's saving work?*

. . . *is there something that shows God's mercy?*

. . . *is there something that shows God's undeserved love or
work for the sake of someone (grace)?*

. . . *is there something said or shown about faith?*

Putting the Word to Prayer

Using your answers from the Law and Gospel questions,
draft your prayers below.

FIRST—INSTRUCTION

Heavenly Father, in what Your Word has taught me, I
have come to know that . . .

SECOND—THANKSGIVING

Gracious and giving Lord, in what Your Word has taught me, I thank You for . . .

THIRD—CONFESSION OF SIN

Merciful and forgiving Lord, in light of what Your Word has taught me, I confess to You that . . .

FOURTH—PRAYER

Holy Spirit and Guide, in light of what Your Word has taught me, grant . . .

God doesn't leave us to our own devices for reading the Bible. We can use one or more parts of the Lord's Prayer to meditate and reflect upon the text to see if and how it is covered in the prayer that Jesus still teaches us all to pray.

Medical doctors have the ability to listen to our symptoms, examine us, and if needed, take tests to identify the likely cause of our problem. If a doctor has found the cause of the symptoms, a course of action will be prescribed, and then consequently the symptoms will go away. Doctors can do all of this because they have a better understanding of the human body, its abilities and its inabilities, and its interaction with age and environment. They know what a healthy body is, what it really needs to be healthy, what would be unhealthy for it, and what would best restore it to health if it were unhealthy. As those conceived and born in sin (Psalm 51:5), we are born sin-sick. We live in bodies and souls that are constantly ravaged by the symptoms of sin. These sin-sick symptoms manifest themselves within us (our sinful nature/ original sin), in the actual sins we commit and in the sins others commit against us. The ultimate symptom of our sin-sickness is death. No earthly doctor can deal with this kind of sickness. God, in His great love, sent His Son to be the great Physician for all mankind. Jesus came to meet and receive our sin-sickness with all its symptoms and all its consequences, from the moment of conception all the way to our rest in the tomb. Through His life, death, resurrection, and ascension for us, Jesus shows Himself to be both our Great Physician and our cure. With the words given in the Lord's Prayer, we find Jesus, the great Physician, writing the prescription for every human to take to their heavenly Father in prayer that He might fulfill it and save us now and in eternity.

An earthly physician's diagnosis begins with our symptoms and progresses back to find the cause of a physical problem. When it comes to our sin-sickness, the diagnosis must begin with something else. Rather than beginning with the symptoms of our sin, we begin by listening to what Jesus prescribes for us in the Lord's Prayer. What Jesus, the Great Physician, prescribes for us to ask the Father in this prayer, shows us what we do not have and what we cannot obtain apart from the Father's giving. Looking behind the petition "Thy Kingdom come" (i.e., salvation in Christ), Jesus shows you something you as a sinner do not have apart from the Father's giving of it.

In teaching us to pray the Lord's Prayer, Christ teaches us to ask the Father for exactly what we need for life in this fallen world and the world to come. Each petition that Jesus prescribes addresses our hidden yet real need. In teaching us to ask these things of the Father, Christ shows us that He is the only pharmacist who can fill what He has prescribed for us.

Luther writes in the Large Catechism: "Here there is included in seven successive articles, or petitions, every need that never ceases to apply to us. Each is so great that it ought to drive us to keep praying the Lord's Prayer all our lives" (III 34). As these needs constantly overwhelm us throughout our earthly lives, so they beset the lives of everyone since Adam and Eve. The entire biblical account is one of the Almighty God diagnosing the needs common to all (Law), prescribing the common cure for us (promises), and filling the common prescription for all (Gospel) in Jesus Christ. This makes each part and petition of the Lord's Prayer an excellent set of lenses through which you can read the Bible. Using the prescribed introduction, one of the petitions, or the closing, enables you to see the sin-sickness the petition asks to be cured and the Lord fulfilling the petition to cure it.

Finding those places in the text that would be covered in some part of the Lord's Prayer, the Holy Spirit will enable you to see where more and more of the accounts of your own life experience are covered by the various parts of the Lord's Prayer. This serves to bring both the biblical text and you under the same prayer that Jesus taught, and both of these under the same Lord Jesus Christ.

To understand how to use any part of the Lord's Prayer to examine what you read in the Bible, we use the Lord's Prayer section from *Luther's Small Catechism with Explanation*. The following excerpts from that book are from each part of the Lord's Prayer and a set of questions developed from each. Using these, you can go back over your Bible reading to look for the answers. You can use these answers as the basis for your own prayers or simply pray the relevant petition of the Lord's Prayer.

The Introduction

Our Father who art in heaven.

What does this mean?

With these words God tenderly invites us to believe that He is
our true Father and that we are His true children, so that
with all boldness and confidence we may ask Him as
dear children ask their dear father. . . .

In Jesus all believers are children of the one Father and
should pray with and for one another. . . .

These words [*who art in heaven*] assure us that our heavenly
Father, as Lord over all, has the power to grant our
prayers. (pp. 180–81)

In what you have read from Scripture, did God demonstrate His fatherly love by what He did or said? If so, how?

Did God demonstrate that He is Lord over all? If so, how?

Did the person(s) demonstrate that they believe God to be their Father by what they did or said? If so, how?

Did the person(s) pray or intercede for others? If so, what was their prayer?

The First Petition

Hallowed be Thy name.

What does this mean?

God's name is certainly holy in itself, but we pray in this petition that it may be kept holy among us also.

How is God's name kept holy?

God's name is kept holy when the Word of God is taught in
its truth and purity, and we, as the children of God, also

lead holy lives according to it. Help us to do this, dear Father in heaven! But anyone who teaches or lives contrary to God's Word profanes the name of God among us. Protect us from this, heavenly Father! . . .

Since God's name is God as He has revealed Himself to us, we cannot make His name holy, but we do pray that He would help us keep His name holy in our lives. . . .

We keep God's name holy

A. when God's Word is taught among us in its truth and purity; . . .

B. when we live according to the Word of God. . . .

God's name is profaned, that is, dishonored,

A. when anyone teaches contrary to God's Word; . . .

B. when anyone lives contrary to God's Word. (pp. 181–83)

In what you have read, was the name of God kept holy by someone living according to the Word of God? If so, how?

Was it kept holy by someone speaking and teaching God's Word truthfully? If so, what is he or she saying?

Was the name of God dishonored—that is, not given the reverence it is due—by someone living contrary to the Word of God? If so, how?

Was it dishonored by someone speaking and teaching something(s) contrary to God's Word? If so, what?

The Second Petition

Thy kingdom come.

What does this mean?

The kingdom of God certainly comes by itself without our

prayer, but we pray in this petition that it may come to us also.

How does God's kingdom come?

God's kingdom comes when our heavenly Father gives us His Holy Spirit, so that by His grace we believe His holy Word and lead godly lives here in time and there in eternity. . . .

The kingdom of God is His ruling as king over the whole universe (kingdom of power), the church on earth (kingdom of grace), and the church and angels in heaven (kingdom of glory). . . .

We do not pray that God's kingdom of power would come, because that is already present everywhere, but we ask God to

A. give us His Holy Spirit so that we believe His Word and lead godly lives as members of His kingdom of grace; . . .

B. bring many others into His kingdom of grace; . . .

C. use us to extend His kingdom of grace; . . .

D. hasten the coming of His kingdom of glory. (pp. 183–86)

In what you have read, did someone ask/pray for God to reign and rule over . . .

. . . some earthly situation/condition? If so, what was it?

. . . some spiritual situation/condition? If so, what was it?

Did God exercise His rule and reign over . . .

. . . some earthly situation/condition? If so, what was it? How?

. . . some spiritual situation/condition? If so, what was it? How?

Did someone specifically speak the Word of God to others or God? If so, what did the person say? How was it responded to?

Did someone repent and seek God's forgiveness and/or mercy?

Was someone's life changed to a more godly way of living? If so, how?

The Third Petition

Thy will be done on earth as it is in heaven.

What does this mean?

The good and gracious will of God is done even without our prayer, but we pray in this petition that it may be done among us also.

How is God's will done?

God's will is done when He breaks and hinders every evil plan and purpose of the devil, the world, and our sinful nature, which do not want us to hallow God's name or let His kingdom come; and when He strengthens and keeps us firm in His Word and faith until we die. This is His good and gracious will.

It is God's will that His name be kept holy and that His kingdom come, that is, that His Word be taught correctly and that sinners be brought to faith in Christ and lead godly lives. . . .

The devil, the world, and our own sinful nature oppose the good and gracious will of God. . . .

We know that the will of God will always be done, but we want God's good and gracious will to be done in our lives. . . .

God's will is done in our lives when

A. He breaks and hinders the plans of the devil, the world, and our sinful nature, which try to destroy our faith in Christ Jesus; . . .

B. He strengthens and keeps us firm in His Word and faith and helps us lead God-pleasing lives; . . .

C. He supports us in all our troubles until we die. (pp. 186–89)

In what you have read, did you see the will of God being done . . .

. . . while some evil plan or purpose of the devil, the world, or someone's own sinful nature (selfishness) was stopped or hindered? If so, what and how?

. . . while someone correctly taught the Word of God?

. . . while someone was helped to live a God-pleasing life according to the Word of God? If so, how was he or she helped?

. . . while someone's faith was strengthened in God's Word? If so, how?

The Fourth Petition

Give us this day our daily bread.

What does this mean?

God certainly gives daily bread to everyone without our prayers, even to all evil people, but we pray in this petition that God would lead us to realize this and to receive our daily bread with thanksgiving.

What is meant by daily bread?

Daily bread includes everything that has to do with the support and needs of the body, such as food, drink, clothing, shoes, house, home, land, animals, money, goods, a devout husband or wife, devout children, devout workers, devout and faithful rulers, good government, good weather, peace, health, self-control, good reputation, good friends, faithful neighbors, and the like. . . .

We pray to God for daily bread, which includes everything that has to do with the support and needs of the body, because Christ wants us to

A.   realize that our entire life and that of everyone else depends on God; . . .

B.   receive all our physical blessings with thanksgiving; . . .

C.   look to God for physical as well as spiritual blessings. . . .

[God provides our daily bread as] He makes the earth fruitful and blesses us with the ability to work for the things we need. . . .

God does not want us to be selfish but to share with those who are unable to work and to include them in our prayers for daily bread. . . .

These words ["this day" and "daily"] teach us not to be greedy or wasteful or to worry about the future but to live contentedly in the confidence that the Lord will give us what we need. (pp. 189–93)

In what you have read, did you see God providing for the earthly physical needs of someone? If so, what did He provide and how?

Did you see someone acknowledge his or her dependence upon God for all things? If so, how?

Did you see someone show mercy to another by providing for that person's earthly needs? If so, what and how did he or she provide for that need?

Did you see someone give thanks to God for what He had done? If so, how did that person thank Him?

Did you see someone call upon God for some earthly need? If so, what did he or she pray for?

The Fifth Petition

And forgive us our trespasses as we forgive those who trespass against us.

What does this mean?

We pray in this petition that our Father in heaven would not look at our sins, or deny our prayer because of them. We are neither worthy of the things for which we pray, nor have we deserved them, but we ask that He would give them all to us by grace, for we daily sin much and surely deserve nothing but punishment. So we too will sincerely forgive and gladly do good to those who sin against us. . . .

We confess that we sin every day and deserve nothing but punishment. . . .

We ask that our Father in heaven would for Christ's sake graciously forgive our sins. . . .

We are not worthy of the things for which we pray and have not deserved them. We therefore need God's forgiveness so that we may pray to Him confidently and in good conscience. . . .

Our heavenly Father wants us to forgive and to do good to those who sin against us. . . .

[When we forgive others,] it shows that we truly believe
that God has forgiven us. (pp. 193–95)

In what you have read, was someone in need of forgiveness? If so, who and for what?

Was the person repentant? How did he or she express it?

Did someone receive forgiveness? If so, from whom:
others or God?

How did the forgiven individual respond?

Was someone forgiving of another?

If so, how did he or she demonstrate that forgiveness?

How did the forgiven respond to the forgiver?

The Sixth Petition

And lead us not into temptation.

What does this mean?

God tempts no one. We pray in this petition that God would
guard and keep us so that the devil, the world, and our
sinful nature may not deceive us or mislead us into
false belief, despair, and other great shame and vice.
Although we are attacked by these things, we pray that
we may finally overcome them and win the victory. . . .

In the Scriptures the words [*tempt* and *temptation*] have two
meanings:

A. The testing of our faith, which God uses to bring us
closer to Himself. . . .

B. The attempts of our spiritual enemies to lure us away
from God and His ways. . . .

The devil, the world, and our sinful nature try to mislead us
into false belief, despair, and other great sins. . . .

> We ask our Father in heaven to give us strength to resist and overcome temptations. (pp. 195–98)

In what you have read, was someone tempted? If so, what was he or she tempted to do?

Who tempted him or her?

Did he or she give into the temptation?

If not, how did he or she overcome it?

If the person did give in, what was he or she deceived or misled by?

In the end, was the person closer to God or further turned away from Him?

The Seventh Petition

But deliver us from evil.

What does this mean?

> We pray in this petition, in summary, that our Father in heaven would rescue us from every evil of body and soul, possessions and reputation, and finally, when our last hour comes, give us a blessed end, and graciously take us from this valley of sorrow to Himself in heaven. . . .

> The seventh petition is a summary petition in which we ask our Father in heaven to rescue us from the devil and all evil which has come into the world because of sin. . . .

> In a world ruined by sin, the Lord keeps us from harm and helps us to endure the troubles that He allows to come into our lives. . . .

> We want our Father in heaven to keep us faithful to Him and when we die to take us from this sorrowful world to Himself in heaven. (pp. 198–200)

In what you have read, was someone in need of rescue from some kind of evil?

Was it evil to body or soul? If so, what was the evil?

Was it evil to possession or reputation? If so, what was the evil?

Did God rescue someone from the devil? If so, who and how?

Did God rescue someone from sin? If so, what sin and how?

Was God keeping someone faithful to Himself? If so, who and how?

The Conclusion

For Thine is the kingdom and the power and the glory forever and ever. Amen.

What does this mean?

This means that I should be certain that these petitions are pleasing to our Father in heaven, and are heard by Him; for He Himself has commanded us to pray in this way and has promised to hear us. Amen, amen, which means "yes, yes, it shall be so." . . .

The word *amen* means "so shall it be" and emphasizes that God, who has commanded us to pray, will hear our prayers and answer them as He has promised. . . .

How do I know God is able to answer the prayers of His people in Christ Jesus?

A.   He alone is the King who has all good gifts in His control. . . .

B.   He alone has the power to grant our petitions. . . .

C.   He has all glory and is worthy of our praise. (pp. 200–201)

In what you have read, did you see God giving good gifts? What was given? Who received it? How did they receive it?

Did God use His power to grant someone's prayer? How did He use His power? Who was blessed by the use of His power?

Was God glorified or praised by those who were blessed by what He gave or did?

Where would you put the "amen"?

Write down what you have learned from your study along with the verse. Looking over this allows you to better apply Luther's four stands and turn it into prayer.

Using The Lens

Using the Second Petition, read Ephesians 2:1–10.

THE SECOND PETITION: THY KINGDOM COME

In what you have read,

Did someone ask/pray for God to reign and rule over . . .

. . . some earthly situation/condition? No. If so, what was it?

. . . some spiritual situation/condition? No. If so, what was it?

Did God exercise His rule and reign over . . .

. . . some earthly situation/condition? No. If so, what was it? How?

. . . some spiritual situation/condition? Yes. *If so, what was it?* I was dead in my trespasses, following the course of this world and the prince of the power of the air, living out the passions of my flesh, carrying out the desires of my body and mind, by nature a child of wrath like everyone else. How? He made me alive together with Christ, by grace He saved me, raised me up with Christ and seated me with Him in the heavenly places in Christ. By grace He has saved me through faith, by His workmanship in Christ Jesus.

Did someone repent and seek God's forgiveness and/or mercy? No. *If so, what was it?*

Did someone specifically speak the Word of God to others or God? No. *If so, what did they say? How was it responded to?*

Did someone repent and seek God's forgiveness and/or mercy?

Was someone's life changed to a more godly way of living? Yes. *If so, how?* I was made dead in trespasses and sin, and He made me alive in Christ Jesus. Since I am now saved by His grace, I must have been lost. I am now His workmanship in Christ Jesus for good works.

While the answers above are by no means exhaustive, they serve to show what using the Second Petition can help you discover when reading the Bible.

Putting the Word to Prayer

When turning your findings into prayer, pray about these things in terms of your needs and thanksgivings. Then go back over and pray these for your family and/or your church. Again, as no one is able to confess the personal sins of another, we do not offer such a confession for our family or congregation. What follows will offer both types of prayer for the first, second, and fourth strands.

INSTRUCTION

(FOR SELF) Heavenly Father, in what Your Word has taught me, I have come to know that by Your grace alone You have saved me from my sin and raised me from being dead in my trespasses to being alive in Christ Jesus. You have taught me that I am Your workmanship in Christ Jesus to do good works. In Jesus' name. Amen.

(FOR FAMILY) Heavenly Father, in what Your Word has taught me, I have come to know that by Your grace alone You have saved my family from their sin and raised them from being dead in their trespasses to being alive in Christ Jesus. You have taught me that each of them is Your workmanship in Christ Jesus to do good works. In Jesus' name. Amen.

THANKSGIVING

(FOR SELF) Gracious and giving Lord, in what Your Word has taught me, I thank You for saving me from my sin and

raising me from death to life in Christ purely by Your grace. Thank You for making me Your own workmanship in Christ Jesus to do good works. In Jesus' name. Amen.

(FOR FAMILY) Gracious and giving Lord, in what Your Word has taught me, I thank You for saving my family from their sin and raising them from death to life in Christ purely by Your grace. Thank You for making each of them Your own workmanship in Christ Jesus to do good works. In Jesus' name. Amen.

CONFESSION OF SIN

(FOR SELF) Merciful and forgiving Lord, in light of what Your Word has taught me, I confess to You that I too often follow the course of this world, living out the passions of my flesh and carrying out the desires of body and mind. I deserve to be nothing but a child of Your wrath. Please forgive me for these sins and all my sin for the sake of Jesus. Amen.

PRAYER

(FOR SELF) Holy Spirit and Guide, in light of what Your Word has taught me, grant me the ability to believe in Jesus Christ and always trust in His saving grace. Lead me to do all works in faith that they may be good in Your sight. All this I ask in Jesus' name. Amen.

(FOR FAMILY) Holy Spirit and Guide, in light of what Your Word has taught me, grant my family the ability to believe in

Jesus Christ and always trust in His saving grace. Lead each of them to do all works in faith that they may be good in Your sight. All this I ask in Jesus' name. Amen.

Key Points

● In teaching us to pray the Lord's Prayer, Christ teaches us to ask the Father for exactly what we need for life in this fallen world and the world to come.

● Each part speaks of what we lack and have no way of obtaining without our heavenly Father's mercy.

● The parts and petitions of the Lord's Prayer comprise an excellent set of lenses through which you can read the Bible.

Discussion

1. Have you ever examined you daily life and vocations in terms of the Lord's Prayer?

2. When reading the Bible, have you ever considered how it relates to the Lord's Prayer?

3. How might this process help turn what you read in the Bible into prayer?

4. How might using this process fill each part of the Lord's Prayer with greater meaning when you pray it?

Action Steps

Read Philippians 2:1–11.

● Use one part or petition of the Lord's Prayer and the questions based on Luther's explanation to study what you have read.

● Turn your answers to the questions into prayer for yourself, your family, and/or your church.

Using the Lens

Use the Third Petition of the Lord's Prayer, "Thy will be done on earth as it is in heaven," to look over the Philippians text above and answer the following questions:

In what you have read,

Did you see the will of God being done . . .

. . . *while some evil plan or purpose of the devil, the world, or someone's own sinful nature (selfishness) was stopped or hindered? If so, what and how?*

. . . *while someone correctly taught the Word of God?*

. . . *while someone was helped to live a God-pleasing life according to the Word of God? If so, how was he or she helped?*

. . . *while someone's faith was strengthened in God's Word? If so, how?*

Putting the Word to Prayer

Using your answers from "Using the Lens," draft your prayers below.

FIRST—INSTRUCTION

Heavenly Father, in what Your Word has taught me, I have come to know that . . .

SECOND—THANKSGIVING

Gracious and giving Lord, in what Your Word has taught me, I thank You for . . .

THIRD—CONFESSION OF SIN

Merciful and forgiving Lord, in light of what Your Word has taught me, I confess to You that . . .

FOURTH—PRAYER

Holy Spirit and Guide, in light of what Your Word has taught me, grant . . .

Seek the LORD while He may be found; call upon Him while He is near; let the wicked forsake His way, and the unrighteous man his thoughts; let him return to the LORD, that He may have compassion on him, and to our God, for He will abundantly pardon. For My thoughts are not your thoughts, neither are your ways My ways, declares the LORD. For as the heavens are higher than the earth, so are My ways higher than your ways and My thoughts than your thoughts. For as the rain and the snow come down from heaven and do not return there but water the earth, making it bring forth and sprout, giving seed to the sower and bread to the eater, so shall My word be that goes out from My mouth; it shall not return to Me empty, but it shall accomplish that which I purpose, and shall succeed in the thing for which I sent it. (Isaiah 55:6–11)

As you read your Bible, you seek the Lord where He may be found. The various ways offered for you to prayerfully read the Bible will help you to call upon Him while He is near in His Word. Each simple tool can draw you a little nearer to the Lord to hear just a bit more of what He is saying and doing.

The blessed part of reading the Bible prayerfully is the Bible itself. The Lord tells you that His Word works differently than any other human words. When I tell my kids to go to bed or clean up their room, you can take odds on whether what

I said should happen will happen. My kids can ignore me or delay in accomplishing the words I spoke to them. God's Word is radically different. When God's Word goes out from the pages of your Bible into your heart and mind, it has to work what His Word says. To read God's Word prayerfully is to pray that the Lord accomplishes His purpose in what you have read.

In all your prayerful study of the Bible, remember that as God's Word it is living and active for you (Hebrews 4:12). Through your prayerful reading of it, it will accomplish the purpose for which God gave it to you.

> Now to Him who is able to do far more abundantly than all that we ask or think, according to the power at work within us, to Him be glory in the church and in Christ Jesus throughout all generations, forever and ever. Amen. (Ephesians 3:20–21)